MONTECITO

California's Garden Paradise

MONTECITO

California's Garden Paradise

Text by Elizabeth E. Vogt
Photographs by Steve Eltinge and Mario E. Quintana
Introduction by Isabelle Greene

MONTECITO
California's Garden Paradise

Text by Elizabeth E. Vogt
Photographs by Steve Eltinge and Mario E. Quintana
Introduction by Isabelle Greene

MIP Publishing
Santa Barbara, California

Design: Adine Maron
Editor: Steve Eltinge
Consulting Editor: Cynthia Anderson
Technical Editing: Ray Sodomka
Copy Editing: Seana Fitt, Marion Lane, Sasha Newborn

Library of Congress Cataloging-in-Publication Data
Vogt, Elizabeth E. Montecito, California's Garden Paradise

ISBN: 0-9617204-9-2

First Edition

This Book Is Dedicated to
the Hundreds of Groundskeepers
Whose Daily Work Has Created a Wonderland

Table of Contents

THE ESTATE GARDENS
Page 41

GARDENS FOR OUTDOOR LIVING
Page 163

NATIVE LANDSCAPES
Page 255

INTRODUCTION

As a young child I was often taken to visit the house my grandfather designed for himself in Pasadena. I remember being awed at the wonderful immense garden space, the cool stone walls, and sloping walks with trellises overhung with roses. Even then, it seemed the best that could be. As an adult, I have those same feelings when I walk into the Gamble House designed by my grandfather. I feel a sense of comfort and peace. It is more than just the superficial quality that things are pretty. It is more evocative than that. It registers that my grandfather took the time to be certain that the proportions are right, that the stairs and doorways are in the right place, that the windows invite the beauty of natural light. It is the recognition that he chose to arrange things in a thoughtful way, that he took care of me and all those others who have ever entered the house.

I have the same feeling about Montecito, a place designed to make life the best it can be. Those who live in Montecito are fortunate recipients of the sensitivity of early planners who took time to do things well. Rather than laying out streets along a grid designed to move people from here to there as fast as possible, they intentionally slowed traffic with winding roads and lanes. They encouraged mass planting of trees which now, in their maturity, provide comfort and seclusion for homeowners and add an element of mystery for those passing by.

The owners who built the great estates in Montecito were participants in this thoughtful

planning. They had made their fortunes elsewhere and migrated west to live the California dream, to enjoy the climate, and to raise their families in an ideal environment. They believed in the value and dignity of the individual and they wanted to express that ideal. For them, Montecito was as close to paradise as one could get. And part of the grandness of old Montecito was the largesse of those people. Their estates were opened to those in the community less fortunate and less wealthy than they. Many were the families who came to picnic on the grand lawns on Sundays, to stroll through the gardens, even to swim in the sparkling pools. It was the good life, centered on respect for fundamental comfort and enduring values.

At first these estate builders were inclined to recreate in California the familiar designs in architecture and land-scaping of the East Coast and Midwest or of Europe. Victorian and Italian architectural influences predominated and the formality of their gardens complemented these

styles. But the advantages of East Coast designs were limited, for the most part, to formal indoor living. Long, cold winters and hot, humid summers were best viewed from the inside out. Architectural elements we Californians now take for granted—large windows and doors opening directly to the outside, or sleeping porches—were experimental in 1900. Bringing the outdoors in was an evolutionary process; architects and owners needed time to get used to the idea that it was safe, even comfortable. Gradually, however, the garden became a natural extension of the house.

After the Second World War many things changed. People could no longer afford to build immense estates and, for those who owned them, maintenance became increasingly difficult. What followed was an unsettled period in Montecito's history. Many of the large, cohesive estates were carved up piecemeal and parcels were downsized. Regrettably, many new owners still thought they should create gardens that looked like the ones belonging to the great estates. Such gardens were designed with little regard for proportion and grace. Certainly no thought was given to plantings appropriate to the land, the climate, or the shrinking supplies of water. Other owners were simply busy raising their families and concerned with more practical things than maintaining a beautiful garden.

In the last ten years a new sensibility has grown in Montecito. There is renewed energy to create fascinating designs, even for small properties. Owners seem willing to experiment and are demonstrating a respect for our limited natural resources, water especially. Where drought-tolerant plants did not fit into the old schemes of vistas with grand lawns, new thinking has come to accept the beauty of native plants and the appeal of integrating them into a variety of garden designs. Some older gardens that were almost lost have been reclaimed, and exciting new properties are being created. Most important, however, Montecito remains a place where creative people have implemented a diversity of

garden styles found nowhere else. The beautiful photographs in this book offer just a sampling of the many wonderful gardens unseen by the public. From extraordinary grounds behind rustic gates to the smallest gardens created with love and care, Montecito remains one of the world's botanical marvels. It has been a privilege for me to work these many years in a place so blessed. 🌿

ISABELLE GREENE

ROSES IN JANUARY

Montecito represents that rare and happy combination where the blessings of nature, enhanced by the efforts of people, have created a landscape of legendary beauty. As a mecca for avid gardeners, it is second to none. The region's mild climate means not only roses in January, but also year-round displays of vibrant color in a wealth of spectacular gardens.

Montecito is nestled in the foothills of the Santa Ynez Mountains a few short miles down the coast from Santa Barbara. With a population of approximately eleven thousand settled into ten square miles of land, Montecito is home to a wide array of unusual shops, excellent restaurants, and numerous fine schools (including two institutes of higher learning). Its local economy is fueled by weekend visitors, as well as daytrippers up from Los Angeles. In summer, especially, the "village" comes to life.

Away from the bustle of its two shopping arteries, residents of Montecito retreat down wooded lanes, often behind gates and stone walls, or behind the dense underbrush that typifies much of the landscape, to the privacy of home. Populated primarily by people who came to escape harsh winters or the stress of urban life, the heart of Montecito is largely hidden from view.

Residents who know it well have a tendency to use only superlatives in describing life in Montecito. It is an extraordinary place to live with its year-round summer. The climate is so mild

that rarely is more than a sweater needed to keep warm, even at night. The views are incomparable; the Santa Ynez Mountains to the north glow pink in the afternoon light, and the Pacific Ocean to the south offers glorious sunsets that silhouette the Channel Islands.

Oh yes, there are periodic water shortages, and when the rains do come, sometimes they are a bit intense. The frost occasionally bites off a promising bud or two, and June mornings may be dampened by the fog rolling in off the Pacific. But these minor discomforts are a small price to pay for living in what many believe is the closest thing to earthly paradise.

Just what are the circumstances that have convened to make Montecito the subject of such glowing reviews? The first is geography. Due to a dramatic curve in the coastal topography just northwest of Santa Barbara, Montecito is situated on the only coastline in the United States running in an east-west, rather than north-south, direction. To the

north (inland), Montecito is sheltered by the Santa Ynez Mountains. This range, which rises to four thousand feet at its highest point, stretches from Ojai in the east to Point Concepcion in the northwest.

As a result of these geographic parameters, Montecito is blessed with what many have described as a true Mediterranean climate. Although Montecito's weather patterns are more diverse than those of the Mediterranean (which generally has two seasons; wet and dry), the climate of Montecito is often favorably compared with that in the south of France, as well as in certain favored areas in Australia, South Africa and Chile.

But geography and climate aren't the whole story. Montecito's reputation as an earthly paradise has as much to do with the diversity of plant life thriving in this relatively small area. Long before early horticulturists introduced exotic plants to Santa Barbara County, the terrain abounded in stands of wild oak and sycamore, orange poppies, wild grape, fruiting cactus and other wonders. The multitude of previously unseen plant forms growing in profusion prompted early explorers to send home glowing reports of this newfound Eden.

It didn't take long for nurserymen to take advantage of the temperate climate for propagation of imported and exotic species. Drawn to the area by its rapidly growing reputation, and inspired by the Mediterranean coastal environment, the nutrient rich soil and an abundance of sunshine, several of the early Santa Barbara and Montecito horticulturists (notably among them Kinton Ralph Stevens, Francesco Franceschi, Charles A. Reed and John Spence) began to specialize in importing and retailing rare plant species. Catalogues of their offerings were disseminated throughout the country. The 1897 catalogue of Francesco Franceschi, for example, boasted fifteen hundred varieties, including cycads, bamboos, vines, trees, shrubs, bulbous materials, and every kind of palm then known to exist.

Among these pioneering nurserymen, the Englishman Kinton Ralph Stevens perhaps had the most enduring influence on the botanical life of Montecito. Stevens was a landscape designer and nurseryman who understood the relationship between the land and its floraculture. After establishing his nursery in 1885, he offered a catalogue of plants for sale, the first issued in California devoted entirely to botanical rarities; tropical and subtropical species, rarely seen before in the continental United States. Stevens is still described as one of the people primarily responsible for the reputation Montecito enjoyed in the late 1890s as one of the world's principal garden spots. By the end of the century, Santa Barbara was fabled to be the place where plants from widely different climates happily congregate, thriving with more vigor than in their native countries.

Following in the footsteps of the early horticulturists, those who have since chosen to settle in Montecito have, for the most part, treated the area with respect. Just as nature's contribution has been important, the people of Montecito have been pivotal in creating and maintaining its stature and reputation as a garden center. At the turn of the century, a new wave of immigrants arrived in Montecito. Eager to escape the bitter winters of the Midwest and East Coast, this group was drawn largely by reports of the healing and restorative powers of the mineral springs of Montecito, which had been luring visitors for several decades. The comparative ease of travel to the West Coast afforded by the completion of the transcontinental railroad (which arrived in Santa Barbara from Los Angeles in 1887), encouraged these early tourists to return time and again.

Increasing numbers of these seasonal visitors were enticed to stay by the year-round Mediterranean climate. Many established second homes and, in some cases, primary residences. Although shielded from the massive land boom that started in the 1880s, changing the face of Southern California forever, Montecito experienced its own mini-boom, which started just before the turn of the century and continued for several decades. The homes built by these new settlers, many of whom were captains of industry and commerce (such people as Armour, Eaton, Swift, Fleischmann), reflected their immense wealth, if not always impeccable taste. Between 1900 and 1930, over three dozen estate residences were built, increasingly in a Spanish or Mediterranean vernacular, in keeping with local history.

Montecito's formal garden history dates from the construction of these grand villas. The estate builders drew on the expertise of local nurserymen and, with the assistance of various designers, they set about creating landscapes in keeping with the scale of their residences. Their gardens were often modeled after those of the grand estates of Europe, but with themes played out using a wider selection of plant materials. As a result of this teamwork, estates of great beauty with outstanding plantings were developed. Given such exotic names as El Mirador, Piranhurst, La

Toscana and Constantia, these homes quickly became the center for society on the central coast of California.

The estate garden period predominated in Santa Barbara from the turn of the century to the beginning of World War II. The first few of these larger gardens were created in the Italian (Mediterranean) style and, later, the Spanish colonial style. The general tenor of the estate gardens changed in the thirties, when local landscape architect Lockwood de Forest created abstract gardens based on the formal qualities of plants themselves, allowing garden design to break free from historical styles.

While the large flamboyant estates were garnering most of the attention, throughout this period dozens of smaller treasures were also built. Interspersed in and around the larger properties, a surprising number of these more compact home sites devoted just as much time and attention to their garden design as did estates occupying much more acreage. The garden styles of these smaller properties, though sometimes retaining the formal design elements of the larger estates, tended to be much more in keeping with the style of the residence they accompanied. Apparently freed from the need to mimic the great estates of Europe, the builders of the small residences introduced a multitude of architectural styles, most of them with remarkable clarity of design. These smaller "estates" include impeccable examples of English Tudor, English country, French Normandy and American Craftsman design (among others) and feature the works of such notable architects as George Washington Smith, Lutah Maria Riggs, Guy Lowell, Carleton Winslow, Bernard Maybeck and Frank Lloyd Wright.

Following World War II, the entire face of garden design in the United States underwent a dramatic change. Once home from the war, home is where Americans wanted to stay. The prevailing social attitude became more inward looking. Entertaining meant inviting friends home rather than dining out. Even people of great financial means took fewer extended trips, and instead found their recreation in their own back yards. The first landscape designer to translate this attitude into garden design was Thomas Church. Taking his cue from the "Southern California lifestyle," Church designed gardens and landscapes meant to be lived in.

The development of Montecito gardens kept pace with this trend. In a sense, this simply meant that garden design in Montecito continued in the direction it already had been going. Historically, even in the formal gardens of Montecito, people lived outdoors more than in their East Coast counterparts. And, as the highways of Southern California improved in the post-World War II era, Montecito's popularity grew as a site for weekend homes, for people coming in from Los Angeles or even San Francisco, after a busy week at work. Suddenly, it was important that gardens made living outdoors as easy and comfortable as living indoors.

Inadvertently, Montecito has developed historical experience in another garden trend that is now becoming the focus of national attention. Whether recreating the formal gardens of Europe, or designing a garden meant for outdoor living, Montecito's landscape architects, starting with Kinton Stevens, have all faced the problem of water scarcity. Drought tolerant and water efficient gardening are not new concepts in Montecito.

Early landscape designers in Montecito went to elaborate lengths to bring water down from the Santa Ynez Mountains to feed the thirsty gardens of the big estates, many of which had acres of lawn to keep green. The intense popularity of the exotic species introduced by the early nurserymen had as much to do with the drought tolerant nature of the plant materials, as it did with their beauty. In a sense, these gardens of the future turn out to be gardens with a past. With generations of experience in working with native and drought tolerant plant materials to draw on,

landscape designers have made Montecito home to some of the most beautiful water-conscious gardens to be found anywhere.

The variety of gardens in Montecito is staggering. No matter what your preference, you are sure to find at least one or two to your liking, and what you find are impeccably maintained. But paradise can be lost. The continued growth and development of Montecito as a mecca of beautiful gardens has not evolved without work and effort. Its citizens have fought tenaciously for limited growth in their community. The issue of sufficiency and allocation of water is always sure to create a heated debate among the locals. Despite the struggles to allocate natural resources, residents wisely have maintained a sensitivity to the importance of the garden.

It has been said that a part of the garden's art is in its ability to stimulate our sight, touch, taste, smell, and hearing. And on the most intimate level, a garden teaches such virtues as patience, faith, gratitude. The gardens of Montecito do all of that, and more. To find a few magnificent gardens in a community this size would not be unusual. But to find dozens and dozens of immaculately maintained properties, gardens lovingly and magnificently guided and nurtured, from the smallest plot to estates of more than twenty acres, is truly a marvel.

One of Montecito's best known estate gardens, Il Brolino, displays an East Coast heritage of lush gardens, statuary and waterscapes.

Nature's landscape along the Romero Canyon trail in the mountains above Montecito. Right: Early morning fog blankets the Pacific Ocean in this view atop the hiking trail at Hot Springs Canyon.

A filigreed gazebo at Ca' di Sopra marks the loading point for a funicular ride into the canyon below.

Warm tones of afternoon light enhance the authenticity of this newer Mexican colonial architecture.

Because of Montecito's temperate climate, this mix of begonia, alyssum (above) and roses (right) will flourish in almost year-round color.

Left: Ranunculi. Above: An artificial waterfall and variety of plantings combine to create this winter nature-scape.

Water-dependent reeds (right) and drought-tolerant cacti and succulents (above), found in gardens less than a mile apart, demonstrate the spectrum of possibilities for plant selection in the Montecito Valley.

Above: The natural affinity between shade-loving ferns and California live oak is seen throughout Montecito. Right: A dense field of Calla lilies from the cutting gardens of Il Brolino.

Left: A carpet of purple blossoms thrives in Montecito's spring climate. Foxglove (above), succulents and roses (inset), found in the same garden, also benefit from the ideal conditions.

THE ESTATE GARDENS

Montecito is a private place. Dense underbrush, an interlocking network of trees, and ribbons of protective stone walls add an element of mystery to stately properties protected from view. From the air, few of Montecito's homes are visible in a sea of almost uninterrupted green.

Anyone familiar with Montecito's present "woodsy" appearance would be surprised by early photographs of the area. Pictures taken at the turn of the century reveal a landscape of sparse vegetation, an open plain punctuated with small groves of trees and light foliage. Montecito presents itself in these early snapshots as an area of open spaces, meadows, and orchards.

The transition from open plain and orchard to secluded woodland began in the early 1900s. Until then, Montecito was only randomly populated. By 1930, however, more than three dozen large estate residences had been built, each strategically positioned to provide views of the Santa Ynez Mountains rimming the north side of Montecito and, for those perched on knolls, to provide views south to the Channel Islands. When first constructed, the majority of these grand residences were easily visible from the road. But soon elaborate gardens were designed to enhance the structures they surrounded, and to increase the privacy of these estates. A surprising number of these gardens have been impeccably maintained through the years, and several are incomparable examples of botanical diversity. ❧

The beautifully restored landscape at La Toscana represents
the ideal in formal estate garden design.

LOTUSLAND

Premier among the grand estate gardens is Ganna Walska's Lotusland. Garden authorities the world over recognize the name Lotusland as synonymous with the avant garde in gardening style: an aesthetically inspired botanical wonderland where color and form are as important as species and varieties.

This acreage in upper Montecito was a wild stretch of undeveloped real estate when horticulturalist Kinton Ralph Stevens acquired it in the latter part of the nineteenth century. Stevens named the property Cuesta Linda (beautiful hill). Combining an interest in the rare and exotic with an uncanny understanding of the plants most adaptable to the Southern California climate, he cultivated many of the specimens still thriving there.

Following Stevens, the property went through a series of owners until Madame Ganna Walska acquired it in 1941. She renamed it Lotusland and immediately set about the work of revitalizing and expanding the gardens started by

Stevens. As legendary as her gardens, this self-proclaimed "enemy of the average" always showed a flare for the dramatic. Madame Walska's passionate vision inspired the complex, colorful and unconventional gardens. Her hope was that the gardens would become "an outstanding center of horticultural significance." Madame Walska's theatrical nature found expression in the diverse and sometimes antithetical themes developed in her carefully designed thirty-seven acres. Although the residence has changed little since she purchased the property, the original Lotusland plantings changed dramatically under her direction.

Lotusland is not just one garden, it is a carefully crafted interlocking network of over a dozen garden "rooms," each housing a separate botanic collection. The creation of Lotusland was meticulously orchestrated so that each garden room offers a different aesthetic or artistic theme. In developing these themes, Madame Walska pursued the creation of her botanical wonderland with a philosophy that "more is better." This philosophy of garden design translated into a program of mass planting for visual effect. Such a self-conscious strategy might seem extravagant, yet one visit to Lotusland is enough to convince anyone that Madame Walska's gardening philosophy works.

The approach to Lotusland sets the scene for more sustained viewing. Its graceful iron portals are filigreed with the outline of the lotus for which the estate was named. Dense green foliage flanks the drive curving toward the interior of the property hinting at mysteries beyond. After the gates swing open, the invitation to explore further is irresistible. For visitors arriving any time from December through February, the path inward is punctuated by the brilliant red torches of a wall of aloe. These flaming sentinels stand above a bed of sedum and are framed by a forest of blue gum eucalyptus and acacias.

Various garden rooms line the path leading to the main residence, starting with the Blue Garden on the right.

In this garden room, each neighboring plant color is associated in a logical progression of color relationships. Reputed to be absolutely magical under a full moon, all of the plantings here are in minor-key shades. Blue Erythea armata palm, Mexican blue fan palm, cedar and blue spruce all provide shade for a carpet of blue furcraeas, blue fescue grass and grey-blue ice plant.

To the left of the main path, through an archway of branches, is a collection of water lily and lotus. This centerpiece of the gardens is growing in what were formerly the swimming pools for the estate. The larger center pond is filled with American and Indian lotus. The two side ponds feature tropical water lilies, papyrus, and horsetail reeds. This group of ponds is surrounded by blue agapanthus and canna lilies, alarmingly red in vibrant contrast to the surrounding deep and lush green foliage.

The path leading from the main gates terminates at the residence, a large California-style stucco house that was approximately twenty years old when Ganna Walska purchased the estate. Nearby, and in sharp visual contrast to the pink of the residence, are a grove of white, hairy cotton candy columns (Neobuxbaumia polylopha), and a grouping of Mexican golden barrel and Brazilian golden ball cactus. Once a small and undistinguished collection, these plants have grown into a veritable regiment. Hundreds of these specimens spill forth as imposing guardians of the residence.

Directly behind this small army is a tangled backdrop of Euphorbia ingens which, though crippled in form, seem to be commanding their assembled neighbors into action. The euphorbia, cactus-like with poisonous, white, milky sap, are of the same genus as poinsettia. These showpiece specimens, some reaching thirty feet high and trailing long, olive-colored tentacles along the stone pavement, wrap up and around the perimeter of the house. Neighboring the euphorbia and cactus is a circular garden of Dracaena draco (Dragon trees) in front of the house. Native to the Canary Islands, the Dracaena draco share their garden room with an unusually fine example of the Chilean Wine Palm. The gathering of specimens for this garden typifies Madame Walska's flamboyant approach to garden design.

The stories of how Madame would direct her chauffeur to take her and her gardener to various nurseries all over Southern California have become legend. On these trips, when some specimen struck her fancy, she would buy not just one or two but dozens of the plant. On one such trip, the hapless chauffeur drove by a residence which displayed a particularly large and beautiful Dracaena draco in the front yard. Madame Walska's reaction, so the story goes, was instantaneous — she had to have the tree. She instructed her chauffeur to approach the owners of the residence and ask how much money they would take to part with their Dragon Tree. At first the owners were unmoved by the strange request. However, Madame Walska offered more and more money, until finally they accepted, and they

sold their tree. This acquisition now stands at the front of the Dracaena draco garden at Lotusland.

To the side of the residence is the first of two bromeliad gardens, displaying several dozen of the hundreds of varieties of bromeliads living on the property. Although thousands of varieties exist, most of them native to South America, the collection at Lotusland provides an excellent assortment. Some display minute white blossoms, some variegated leaves, others deep and vibrant cardinal or purple centers, and still others torch-like blossoms from a base of deep green. All take sustenance from rain and dew captured by their leaves and flower cups.

At the heart of the estate is the great lawn, at the edge of which is a spectacular Monterey cypress standing well over one hundred feet tall. The site where the cypress now grows formerly was the location of a large lath house used by Kinton Stevens to store his exotic specimens until they were either sold or planted somewhere on the estate. Among

them was a juvenile cypress. Forgotten and unplanted, the hardy tree matured, eventually splitting the roof of the lath shelter. Ultimately, the lath house was torn down to accommodate the tree, which is now more than a hundred years old.

Beyond the cypress at the edge of the main lawn, and partially hidden from view, sits one of the most amusing of the many surprises Lotusland offers: a large, mechanical, topiary clock. This twenty-five-foot timepiece, created in 1955 by Ralph Stevens for the National Shade Tree Convention, has a face of gravel and blue-grey ice plant. Surrounding the clock is a collection of topiary figures. Created from eugenias, junipers, and cypress, these droll creatures include a goose, seal, duck, rabbit, elephant and a large dinosaur with iron teeth and light bulbs for eyes.

The path out of the topiary garden leads across the back lawn and into another imaginary playground. This time the theme is a theatrical one. Surrounded by a grove of

"ponytail palms," which are not really palms at all despite their swollen elephantine feet and ponytail headdresses, is a bizarre collection of concrete statues of little people. Madame Walska is said to have given operatic concerts for this very private, and very attentive, audience.

An exit at the back of the "theater" leads to the succulent garden. These plants, which always seemed to be the most boring when grown individually in grandmother's garden, take on an entirely different character when planted en masse. The garden is arranged with a careful eye for size, color, shape and texture. The groupings presented here, of succulents both rare and commonplace, create miniature tableaux of surprising beauty.

Near the succulent area is one of the most unusual collections of Lotusland. The cycad garden is laid out on small, grassy hillocks around a koi pond, and was planned by Madame Walska when she was in her eighties. Considered to be the most important botanical collection of

Lotusland, these cycads are native to Mexico, Australia, Japan, South Africa, Florida, the Caribbean, and South America. The cycad collection at Lotusland includes approximately one hundred and thirty of the one hundred and fifty known varieties in the world, and includes some species no longer found in the wild. Madame Walska bought many of the rarest of her cycads from a botanical garden in England. Others were propagated from seed as well as from "pups" in the Lotusland greenhouse. The "homegrown" cycads include Encephalartos woodii, of which no females are in existence.

The final major "room" of Lotusland is the Japanese garden. Appropriately, the entry is through a torii gate. Set in a basin, the Japanese garden is buffered from the surrounding gardens by a wreath of Japanese red maples, heavenly bamboo, Japanese black pines, Japanese cedar and the gingko or maidenhair tree.

At the heart of the Japanese garden is a large pond,

constructed during the early days of the property, and presently dedicated to the propagation of water lily and lotus. Rimming the pond, just inside the buffer zone of maple, cedar, and pine, are clusters of Tulip magnolia trees. There also is an imposing wall of camellias, including Camellia japonica and Camellia sasangua. Blooming profusely in February and March, the magnolia and camellia in multi-hued pinks, variegated reds, and creamy whites, convey the sense of abundance that epitomizes all the gardens of Lotusland.

The newest addition to the Japanese garden is a pavilion, which joins a collection of other shrines, including stone lanterns and pagodas. Each shrine serves a symbolic purpose as well as a decorative one. The small round lantern in the pond represents a lighthouse, while other lanterns are for donations to Buddha. In addition to being decorative, the five-tiered pagoda represents the five elements—sky, wind, fire, water and earth; and the five cardinal virtues— humanity, justice, politeness, wisdom and fidelity.

The gardens of Lotusland are extraordinary. Words cannot convey the beauty and complexity of this experiment in adventurous gardening. Realizing the transitory nature of existence, Ganna Walska extended the limits of current horticultural practice to create something enduring. In doing so, she has provided generations to come with a botanical workshop of undeniable beauty and importance. ❧

Graceful iron portals at the entrance of Lotusland are filigreed with the outline of the lotus for which the estate was named. Right: Red-torched aloe, foreground, grow near the shell-rimmed pool, a favorite creation in Ganna Walska's Aloe garden.

Left: A regiment of Mexican golden barrel cacti spill forth as imposing guardians of the residence. Above: In contrast to the lushness that typifies Lotusland, the simplicity of this desert-like scene outside Ganna Walska's residence illustrates her fondness for diversity.

Clustered specimens of mature Neobuxbaumia polylopha represent Madame Walska's philosophy of mass planting for visual effect .

Many of the drought tolerant species bloom infrequently. *The flowering foot-like tentacle of the Euphorbia ingens (above) blooms annually, and the torch-like blossom (right) of the Agave americana (Century plant) signals the end of the plant's life.*

The bromeliad garden at the edge of the great lawn displays an excellent cross section of the multiple varieties found at Lotusland.

Filtered light plays off the variety of plantings in this ground level view of the fern garden. Left: This Jacobean musician, set against a backdrop of Podocarpus gracilior, was brought to Lotusland from Ganna Walska's French estate and is one of several that adorn the tiered seating area of the theater where she gave private operatic concerts.

Cycads are are considered to be premier among the important botanical collections at Lotusland.

The delicate flowering Tulip magnolia tree bordering the pond of the Japanese garden blooms in profusion each spring.

Koi and water lilies thrive in the Japanese pond created from a reservoir used by the former owner to collect rainwater. Right: The distant bath house is the only reminder that this stunning lotus pond was once a swimming pool.

The lotus pond in the Japanese garden.

LA TOSCANA

Another of the great estate gardens which demonstrates attention to detail, as well as distinctive style and design, is the impeccably groomed landscape of La Toscana. This garden, nestled in the foothills of the Santa Ynez Mountains, is testimony to the extraordinary amount of time and attention it takes to sustain an enduring garden masterpiece.

The gardens at La Toscana were originally planned in 1927 by A. E. Hanson to provide a backdrop for the estate's residence designed by George Washington Smith, a noted local architect. Hanson's first step was to become intimately familiar with the property, and then to draft a detailed set of plans from which he could direct the creation of the gardens. His plans were so elaborate, the first set of drawings took over a month to complete.

Hanson was inspired by Renaissance gardens he had seen in Italy, particularly the gardens of the Villa Gamberaia near Florence. His drawings called for a series of interlocking garden rooms. Each garden chamber was intended to be a natural extension of the bordering room of the villa and was to have a complementary use, in keeping with the formal themes of Italian Renaissance garden design.

It has been said that without constant care and attention, a garden rapidly reverts to a wild state. A year of neglect can take many years to correct. Such was the case with the gardens of La Toscana. When the current owners arrived at the property, little of Hanson's original work was at first apparent. The grounds were intensely overgrown, with few visual clues to remind them of the exquisite gardens La Toscana was once reputed to possess. So overgrown was the property that the owners' first instinct was to send in a bulldozer to eradicate what remained. Luckily, discretion prevailed and, instead, one man was dispatched with a machete to slice cautiously through the acres of tangled foliage. This intuition was well-rewarded. As the lone gardener patiently stroked through the undergrowth, treasures appeared—Greco-Roman statuary and fountains, and the remains of a network of garden paths.

Convinced they had uncovered something of importance, the owners soon located a copy of Hanson's original plans. Armed with this set of blueprints, they started literally from the bottom up. Before replanting could be undertaken, over four hundred tons of debris had to be removed. The soil throughout the estate was so depleted of nutrients, thirty inches of topsoil was dug up and carted away. In its place, over two hundred tons of manure, mixed with fresh black earth and other fertilizers, re-topped the land.

One of the first areas to be refurbished was the entrance-way and forecourt. The drive into the estate, connecting the main road to the front door, is a straight road, bordered by walls of pittosporum. This arrangement creates the effect of passing through a tall green corridor. At the end of the driveway is the forecourt, which opens out expansively in a circle with a central fountain spurting a stream of water from an ornamental spout.

To the south, the view from the library of the villa leads across "the great English lawn," as Hanson referred to it, and to columns marking the commencement of a pathway. This path provides access to an adjoining chamber, one of the most secluded rooms in Hanson's interpretation of Italian garden architecture. Symmetry is the dominant theme of this garden, which consists almost exclusively of an elaborate parterre of English boxwood. In the middle sits a white pergola with a filigreed iron dome, loosely resembling a miniature Roman temple. Devoid of flowers, this giardino segreto, or secret garden, nevertheless conveys a deep sense of tranquility.

The livingroom and gallery portions of the villa at La Toscana face eastward, through the loggia and across the patio, to additional garden rooms. These garden rooms were designed to complement the home and provide a fitting backdrop for entertaining and gracious living. Below the

patio, Hanson designed a four-square parterre garden with tapered edges. The shape of the parterre was designed to echo the architecture of the residence itself, right down to the circle of boxwood in the middle repeating the curve of the patio steps. This parterre is particularly effective because it was built to the scale of the house.

The north face of La Toscana provides a view of the Santa Ynez Mountains. The garden Hanson designed for the northern plane of the estate further exemplifies his interest in architectural references. It is a symmetrical collection of low parterre edgings, recalling the shape of the parterre in the east-facing garden. Each parterre is interspersed with a stunning array of a different shade in a series of multi-hued roses. A path bisects this garden. Commencing at the edge of the terrace, and continuing in the direction of the Santa Ynez range, the path invites the eye outward and upward, thus extending the flow of the house.

As with Renaissance estates, the inherent beauty of the gardens of La Toscana lies in the interrelationship of the parts. The architectural symmetry of long passageways and neighboring parterres, the juxtaposition of open spaces with hidden private areas, and the use of flowers and statuary to punctuate views and provide focus—all are the product of careful planning.

Although Hanson's vision for the gardens at La Toscana was undeniably important, the present beauty of this property must also be credited, in no small measure, to the Herculean efforts of the current owners. They view La Toscana as a work in progress, with plans for continued improvement. Through their patience and hard work, these owners are transcending Hanson's original vision, and adding to the beauty of the original design.

One of George Washington Smith's most beautiful commissions was the residence at La Toscana. In this view, holiday poinsettias brighten the residence entrance in the forecourt.

A classic element of the Italian Renaissance garden was the giardino segreto (secret garden) which was used for meditation and private meetings by clergy and aristocracy. Surrounded by Victorian boxwood, and shaded by Ficus microfila and California live oak, this pristine recreation has been groomed to near perfection.

Above: Roman statues at the end of the patio mark the axial path leading through the rose parterre gardens. Like all of La Toscana, this garden is the result of a commitment made by its owners to renovate and preserve the heritage of this amazing property. Right: Terra-cotta pots planted with citrus are an authentic feature of the Italian parterre garden.

Early morning light accentuates the geometric precision of Japanese boxwood parterres.

Much of the statuary at La Toscana was found buried under years of neglected growth. Once discovered, the current owners restored these treasures and placed them throughout the property.

To the south, the view from the library of the villa leads across "the great English lawn." In the foreground are the bright orange blossoms of the Flame vine.

Landscape maintenance of this expansive property is a never ending process. Workmen seen from this rooftop view attend to the time consuming task of caring for hundreds of specialty rose bushes.

IL BROLINO

The garden themes of Renaissance Italy found a somewhat different expression at Il Brolino. Surrounding an Italianate residence designed by George Washington Smith, the formal gardens of Il Brolino were originally cultivated in 1923 under the watchful eye of landscape architect Florence Yoch. Prior to Il Brolino, Yoch's gardens had been created principally in Hollywood and Beverly Hills for various movieland figures, but a trip to Italy inspired her to create more formal gardens.

As with La Toscana, Il Brolino's landscape consists of a series of garden rooms, connected by terraces and passageways. The linked garden spaces draw the visitor through an almost maze-like progression of garden attitudes, culminating in an immense lawn which spreads out below the rear, or southern face, of the property. Reining in the view across this lawn, and bisected by a path lined with Sweetheart roses, is a magnificent stand of oak. Partially hidden behind these oaks is a rectangular reflecting pool adorned with a Romanesque statue. This elegant and architecturally determined pond of water lilies provides a subtle reminder of these gardens' formal references. A series of stone benches under the oaks invite the garden visitor to rest and enjoy the breathtaking view toward the residence.

The signature statement of the gardens at Il Brolino is undeniably the topiary garden. This area has been enhanced and expanded since Yoch's early design, so that today this parterre is a whimsical wonderland of topiary ingenuity. The principal characters in this cast of topiary figures are birds enjoying their topiary bird baths in all manner of poses, including one particularly free spirit with its tail-end thrust heavenward. The topiary bathing fonts are in turn positioned next to bordering parterres of Japanese boxwood, trained into the shape of four playing cards. The cards, representing the ace of each suit, lend further testimony to the playful intent of this stylized garden display.

At the back of the topiary garden is a stone arch framing a statue of the huntress Diana, inviting the viewer's gaze to include the Santa Ynez Mountains beyond. Framing the view while moving from one garden room to the next seems to have been a conscious endeavor in Yoch's design. This technique was useful in much of her later work designing landscape sets for motion pictures. She also shows a keen recognition and appreciation of the varied landscape of Montecito. Except for the eastern border of this property abutting the roadway, in every other direction the views from these gardens are spectacular. To the north, the view is of the ever-changing mood and temperament of the Santa Ynez Mountains. From pale ocher, through peach to deep rust, each of the hues projected by the Santa Ynez range finds its complement in the subtle tones and shadings used by Yoch in her garden palette. To the south and southwest is a view of the Pacific Ocean, and, on a clear day, an unobstructed view of the Channel Islands.

The subtle art of making formal garden themes approachable enlivens each of the garden rooms at Il Brolino. The western face of the residence is adorned with a sunken garden—a private meditation room without the formal walls of a more traditional Renaissance garden. There is still the sense of privacy and separation from the rest of the estate, yet with a subtle set of defining cues. Looking out from this garden, the viewer may notice that the angles are not quite set; everything seems a bit off center. Yoch's style often offset the symmetry of a garden by a misplaced statue, bench, or a tree that interrupts the extended view.

Formality and intimacy. Form and substance. The gardens of Il Brolino invite such studies in apparent opposites which some may say is the very substance of which Montecito is made. ❧

Iceland Poppy. Right: The club in the foreground and diamond behind are two of the four aces in the topiary garden. The dark leaved and cone shaped Waxleaf privet add contrast to the light green Japanese boxwood.

Well known for her work as a set designer in Hollywood, in 1923 Florence Yoch applied her landscape talents to the original styling of the grounds at Il Brolino.

MIRAFLORES

Although Montecito once boasted several dozen grand estates with elaborate gardens, less than half of them have withstood the ravages of time, and this number continues to dwindle. One property that has survived in a most creative way is the estate known as Miraflores (Look at the Flowers), home to the Music Academy of the West.

Few of Montecito's other estates have had a more charmed or eclectic life. The main building of Miraflores, a large stucco villa (variously described as Mexican-styled or Mediterranean-styled), is set on a knoll above the beach and was originally designed by Francis W. Wilson as the third clubhouse of the Santa Barbara Country Club, a function it serve from 1909 to 1917. In 1917, the property was sold to John and Mary Jefferson who hired architect Reginald Johnson to make the changes necessary to transform the property from a clubhouse to a spacious private residence. The remodeling took twelve months during which time extensive formal gardens were designed by Paul G. Thiene.

For thirty years the Jeffersons enjoyed the privileges of living on one of Montecito's most beautiful properties. When Mary Jefferson died in 1950, she left a large monetary gift to her personal secretary, Helen Marso, who used the money to purchase Miraflores from the estate. Like the Jeffersons, Ms. Marso was an avid music lover and donated the residence and estate property to the then fledgling Music Academy of the West. Prior to Ms. Marso's gift, the Academy had no permanent home, but was already building a substantial reputation for fine instruction. Classes taught by such distinguished artists as Darius Milhaud, Arnold Schoenberg, Gregor Piatigorsky and Igor Stravinsky helped attract promising students from across the United States.

Through the years, the fame and success of the Music Academy has grown substantially, providing Santa Barbara with a musical institution that now rivals Juilliard School in New York and Curtis Institute in Philadelphia. Today, enrollment includes students from eighteen countries. In recognition of the importance of fostering future musicians and fine musicianship, its endowment provides scholarship awards for ninety percent of all students.

Although the life of Miraflores revolves around music, the Directors of the Academy have not lost sight of the relationship between pristine surroundings and the creation of beautiful music. Great care has been taken to maintain the park-like wooded grounds which provide an ideal setting for students to escape from the world and develop their talents. Because of its special location and cultivated beauty the Academy also serves as a setting for weddings and other special community events.

It is not unusual for visitors to find one or more students practicing near the classic reflecting pool, a special area of peace and tranquillity. The back of the former residence offers another special view across a large clear pool, vine-covered trellises, Butterfly Beach and beyond to the ocean. Numerous paths lace the grounds, some terminating in small sanctuaries furnished with statuary, urns, and tile-adorned meditation benches. The property continues to evolve through expansion and renovation. New landscaping includes the imaginative use of native plants and succulents indicating a forward looking decision to maintain the garden heritage of Miraflores in balance with concerns for water resources.

Left: Musical cherubs greet visitors to the gardens at Miraflores. Above: The serenity of the formal reflecting pool draws students who seek a tranquil place to practice.

A heavily-laden trellis of golden Copa de Oro, stands adjacent to the sparkling pool below the eastern terrace.

This classical garden is a frequent site for garden weddings.

ARMOUR ESTATES

In 1916, Lolita Armour and her husband, J. Ogden Armour (heir to the famous Chicago meat packing business), acquired the first sixteen acres of what was to become a seventy-acre estate at the upper end of Cold Springs Road. Under Ms. Armour's guidance, and with the assistance of landscape architect Elmer Awl, Ms. Armour set about the task of landscaping her extensive property.

In the 1920s, the Armours' daughter, also named Lolita, and her husband John J. Mitchell Jr. took over the task begun by Lolita's mother, and devoted themselves to continuing the development of this estate, known as El Mirador. A grand scheme for the property was envisioned. An elegant residence and accompanying gardens were to occupy the central fourteen acres of the property, with magnificent views of the Santa Ynez Mountains on one side and the Pacific Ocean and the Channel Islands on the other. Plans also included a complete Provençal village.

With Awl's direction, the estate's formal gardens were essentially completed by 1925. However, the residence to accompany them was never built. The Mitchells divorced in 1941, and for much of the intervening period the gardens sat abandoned and neglected.

More recently, the Armour acreage has been divided into several parcels, and much of the Estates' gardens have been restored to their former glory.

El Mirador

Today the portion of the Armour Estates that retains the name "El Mirador" is occupied by an heir of the original owners. The long, beautiful drive that forms the entrance to the property passes the original gatehouse, one of the few reminders on this property of the Provençal village planned by Lolita Mitchell.

At the center of this portion of the former estate sits the ghostly foundation of "Riso Rivo," the residence of Charles Eaton, who sold the property to the Armours.

Though the upper wooden portion of the residence burned in the early 1920s, stone columns identifying the parameters of the first floor remain. A lovely garden of wild annual chrysanthemum and impatiens has grown among the ruins. Adjacent to the Eaton ruin, steps lead down to a stone grotto which once provided a shady, fern-covered retreat. Nearby, the ruins of a wisteria arbor can still be seen.

The grounds of El Mirador also include a refurbished Japanese garden with koi ponds and a small drought tolerant garden. On the site of the estate's original walled rose garden, a grassy plot is now bordered by colorful flowers and enhanced by the music of a lovely rock waterfall.

The Robert Webb Estate

Meticulously recreating and recapturing the feel of Elmer Awl's original design, the gardens of the Robert Webb Estate on the upper acreage of the former Armour Estates are a breathtaking reminder of an era when fantasy was the stuff of which everyday life was made.

The entrance to the gardens is on a knoll, at the point where the Mitchells' great residence was to be built. Two terra-cotta griffins mark the start of a pathway which descends some five hundred feet toward a succession of distinct garden areas. The highest of the areas, bisected by a terraced walk, is a formal Italian garden. Connecting water channels highlight each level of this terraced masterpiece, reminiscent of Moorish water gardens.

Matching sets of boxwood parterres line the pathway on each side of the descending water staircase. These geometrically precise plantings echo the linear message conveyed by the pathway and the water channels. Emerging from the mirrored parterres are a collection of rose bushes and a grove of Deodar cedars. The spontaneity of the cedar grove, juxtaposed with the precision of the parterre, creates an enchanting illusion.

At the base of the terraced steps is a sunken lotus

pond. This beautiful reflective pool, embedded in an open grassy plateau, is adorned with cherubic statuary. As the viewer turns from the pool to gaze upward toward the twin griffins at the head of the garden, there is a special moment as one realizes that the parterres lining the path, the double set of giant cedars, and the palm trees flanking the entrance to the garden provide a perfect visual framing for Montecito Peak.

The final garden area on this axis consists of a large open English lawn, rimmed with flowering beds of annuals and perennials. One could easily envision a leisurely game of croquet in progress.

Adjacent to these interconnected garden areas, but set off in a small canyon, is an outdoor amphitheater. In years gone by, this theater hosted performances by groups such as the Chicago Symphony Orchestra. From this venue an exceptional vista opens up across treetops to the ocean and islands beyond.

Above the amphitheater and nestled in a small forest is perhaps the most unexpected surprise in this garden of many surprises: a small cascading waterfall that winds its way down through a series of boulders and stream rocks to a pond. This pond is home to a collection of Chilean and African Greater flamingoes, who spend their time idling in dappled sunlight filtered through the overhanging branches. From the pond, a camouflaged trail proceeds through a wooded, almost jungle-like glen, home to a collection of tropical birds. Each variety of bird is housed in a separate aviary, crafted to blend into the background. This jungle-like area features immense staghorn ferns emerging from the ells of neighboring trees, as well as hostas, orchids and palms.

The diversity within these fourteen acres is astounding. The spectacular gardens of the Robert Webb Estate serve as an important reminder of the significance of this property in the social history of Montecito.

Villa Lilybelle

A third subdivision of the Armour Estates is Villa Lilybelle. This exceptional estate combines historical and contemporary elements to create a serene atmosphere. The long entry drive passes a tree-shaded reservoir originally built by Charles Eaton. Between the reservoir and the residence are reminders of the exotic palm tree grove planted over seventy years ago for Lolita Armour.

The old adobe (part of the original Provençal village) which now serves as a pool house, adjoins a lush rose garden and the swimming pool area. The spacious main residence is newly built on the site of the old kitchen/dining area dating back to the original Armour estate.

Among the newer additions to this property is an exquisite walled meditation garden, planted exclusively with variations of snow-white blossoms and grey-green leaves. Here, as in other garden areas of Villa Lilybelle, the property's fabled heritage is sensitively reflected.

The fern grotto designed by Robert Webb is home to several species of rare tropical birds, including these African Greater flamingos.

Like the property itself, white swans summon images of a bygone era.

Emerging from matching sets of parterres are a collection of rose bushes as well as a series of Italian cypress, some reaching thirty feet or more.

The informality of arching magnolia branches counterpoints the precision of the highly groomed rose garden below. Left: Delicate ferns thrive in this mini-tropical forest as a near authentic native environment for these South American conures.

This idyllic scene at the foot of a majestic stand of Deodar cedars offers an inspired setting for meditation.

Lolita Armour's dream home was to have been built opposite the octagonal pond which marks the entrance to the gardens below.

Montecito Peak, framed by Washingtonian palms, stands in the background of the terraced water garden.

Subdivision of the Armour estate created several prime parcels upon which newer estate properties, such as Villa Lilybelle, have been developed. The view from the balcony (above) opens out to terraced lawns and the remains of Lolita Armour's palm garden which, at one time, included rare specimens from around the world. The new Mediterranean style residence (right) was designed in conformity with the property's heritage.

Wild annual chrysanthemum, impatiens and fern grow in abundance among the stone ruins of the original Eaton house (Riso Rivo) destroyed by fire in the 1920s and never rebuilt. Left: Lush branches of the Chinese elm provide shade cover for water plants and koi that live in several of the estate ponds.

A number of ponds and reservoirs in the estate gardens have become refuges for migratory birds. This mallard is one of several wild ducks that have made El Mirador a permanent home.

A backlit catalpa branch frames a portion of the sunken walled garden. Originally surfaced in Mediterranean colors, years of dampness and shade have changed the patina to grey and off-white.

CASA BIENVENIDA

Although many of the large estate gardens in Montecito embrace formal European design themes, no two present them in the same way, or with the same degree of loyalty. Some, such as La Toscana, adopt these themes in a studied and formal manner. Others, such as El Mirador, adapt the themes to the needs of the property owner, interweaving formal design elements with a sense of wonder. One garden that presents these same Renaissance themes with an almost theatrical vision is Casa Bienvenida.

At Casa Bienvenida there is an air of studied insouciance in a landscape strewn with Italian vernacular. Even the name Casa Bienvenida, which means "House of Welcome ," implies an impish theatricality. The residence, an extravagant structure abounding in Spanish and Moorish references, was designed and built in 1930 by Addison Mizner. No expense was spared, despite the fact that the country was in the middle of the Great Depression. When Lockwood de Forest was commissioned to create formal gardens on the seventeen

acres surrounding the estate, he also was allowed an unlimited budget.

Casa Bienvenida is nestled into a series of gently undulating slopes, and Lockwood de Forest took this into account. Starting with dramatic Italian water gardens on the north face of the property, de Forest used the slope to his advantage. Historically, water channels are said to represent the passage of time, but one gets the impression that the passage of time was not the designer's primary concern in this most unconventional of gardens.

The water channels of Casa Bienvenida are nearly exact replicas of the water cascade at the Villa Lante in Bagnaia, Italy. Each water channel is a connected series of bowls or shells, the edges of which form a lazy "S" pattern. Each bowl is tipped slightly to allow the water to splash over its lip and into the shell below, and so on down the pathway until the water is diverted underground at the base where the two channels meet at the patio of the residence.

The channels are flanked by terra-cotta urns, with citrus trees and rows of Italian cypress standing guard. Water channels are often used in garden settings to animate what might otherwise be a rather predictable garden space and at Casa Bienvenida the water channels are most dramatic.

At the top of the parallel cascades is a stone Palladian-style structure, designed as a tea house, placed on its own stone fortress. Into a niche in the face of the stone fortress is set an ornate fountain in the semblance of a neoclassic shrine. The tea house is guarded by statuary of Roman goddesses.

At the base of the water channels is a terrace bordered with rows of yellow hibiscus bushes. The terrace is home to immense oversized stone chalices and a large stone bathtub. The sense of melodrama continues as the plantings framing the side of the house draw the eye up toward a number of stone gargoyles. The terrace is also home to other architectural embellishments, including elaborate ironwork around the windows and on the side of the house, echoing the Spanish/Moorish themes of the architecture.

The second half of the formal gardens of Casa Bienvenida is located on the eastern side of the residence. It begins at the base of a hillside covered with agave, aloe, and jade plants, all nestled in and around outcroppings of indigenous rock. A path winding down through this wooded garden of muted greens and silver-blue meanders through a grove of olive and eucalyptus, then on to the geometrically precise second major set of formal gardens.

This garden area consists of a trio of rose gardens, each set into an intricately designed parterre. Each of the three is separated by a hedge, approximately ten feet tall and running the perimeter. From the air, the layout of these gardens echoes precisely the architectural theme of the Palladian-style tea house at the top of the water channels with its three openings separated by two columns. The central rose garden has a curved finial, repeating the arching motif of the central portion of the tea house; and two side rose gardens are truncated at the end, mimicking the two side portals to the tea house, which are flat across the top. In addition, pillars stand like sentinels along the sides of each portion of the rose garden, each connected at the top to the next by a great looping chain. These pillars recall those on the face of the tea house, with the additional theatrical touch of the connecting metal links. The Palladian architectural theme of the rose gardens is finally played out in the pergola at the eastern edge, echoing the roofline of the tea house. Although arguably dramatic to the point of affectation, the consistency of themes is fully in keeping with the architectural statement made by the residence. These rose gardens demonstrate why Lockwood de Forest was frequently described as a designer of vision and genius.

On the south side of the property is an expansive stone patio bordered by a balustrade consisting of rows of small pillars. The steps down from the patio are flanked by statuary of Roman maidens, and lead onto a wide sloping lawn. Against the complexity and visual activity of the water garden and the rose parterres, this long slope of green is balm for the eyes. The patio itself, bordered by the silver-green of neighboring eucalyptus and stands of oak and cedar, balances the intensity and energy of the other garden areas. This aesthetic balance makes the gardens of Casa Bienvenida successful. Dramatic and theatrical? Perhaps. But the drama harmonizes with the architectural themes presented by the residence, ingeniously balanced by the open formality of the great lawn and the relaxed informality of the wooded hillside laced with footpaths. At Casa Bienvenida, Lockwood de Forest aggressively adapted Renaissance gardening themes not only to the architecture presented, but also to the land itself, maintaining a sense of dignity and proportion throughout. 🌿

Delicate leaves of lemon-scented gum are illuminated behind one of many Moorish vases adorning the balcony to the great lawn.

Designed after the water gardens of Villa Lante in Bagnaia, Italy, the water channels of Casa Bienvenida (above) flow from the Palladian tea house to the patio. December raindrops coat these Agave americana adjacent to a jade plant in full bloom (right).

Intricate parterres, chain-laced columns and the extensive use of statuary are characteristic of Lockwood de Forest's flamboyant style.

Garden motifs are played out in the iron gates of the Palladian tea house.

Addison Mizner designed Casa Bienvenida in 1930. The estate (above) features Moorish influences (right) and intricate pediments.

LAS TEJAS

Ornamental water gardens are the most striking element at Las Tejas, one of the oldest Montecito estates. The name Las Tejas means "the tiles," and the property is aptly named; its roofing tiles are almost all that remains on the residence from 1898, the date it was built. Constructed originally as a Mission-style adobe and roofed with old red tiles taken from abandoned Spanish homes, the property was radically transformed in 1917 into an Italian villa under the guidance of new owner Helen (Mrs. Oakleigh) Thorne. In transforming the old adobe, local architect Francis W. Wilson drew inspiration from Giacomo da Vignola's 16th-century Villa Farnese built for Cardinal Allesandro Farnese, at Caprarola outside Rome. Among the features Wilson employed to recreate a formal Italian estate are a loggia and a trio of arches, supported by Italianate columns.

To complement the new architecture, Ms. Thorne, who was experienced with surveying and garden tools,

designed her own Italian gardens with Wilson's help. The first garden she planned for Las Tejas was her stunning chain of water basins below the loggia on the garden front. Consisting of a series of three round fountains, each spills water off a scallop shell onto the next succeeding fountain, culminating in a reflecting pool. Roman statuary and urns placed around the fountains further reflect the estate's Italian influence.

Below the pool is a series of stylized lawns, bordered with large hedges. The final pool rests next to an Italianate pavilion, which doubles as a bathhouse, a design concept of Ms. Thorne. In creating her gardens Ms. Thorne was interested in garden architecture as well as plants. She was just as comfortable working with bricks and mortar, rock and soil as she was with planting materials. Her creativity, coupled with her ease with materials, resulted in an unusual "Roman garden": a series of fifteenth-century columns from southern France connected by brick arches and surrounded by a grove of olive trees. Echoing the architectural embellishments of the residence, this quiet stone gazebo serves as a quiet garden sanctuary.

By the time Ms. Thorne was finished, the gardens of Las Tejas covered twenty-six acres. Many of the original garden areas she created have disappeared with the passage of time, including her knot garden of boxwood and pebbles, and an extensive Japanese garden. Those that remain include not only the classical eye-stopping water gardens but also the Spanish walled and tiled garden. The latter was designed with the assistance of George Washington Smith and bears a great similarity to gardens he created at Casa del Herrero. The rose garden and the Roman garden also remain. Additional garden areas have been added in recent years, the most notable being a native landscape created around a revitalized stream bed in an area of the property that had been a wooded terrace. 🌱

Elegant bronze sculptures, of two nymphs, a satyr and Pan, brought to Las Tejas by Oakleigh and Helen Thorne, pose in front of the residence.

Seventy-five years of growth have partially obscured the trio of arches and loggia, signature features for which Las Tejas is famous. As a function of enduring vision, Helen Thorne's garden design remains as inspiring today as it was in 1917.

The stunning chain of water basins below the loggia consist of a series of three round fountains; each spills water off a scallop shell into the next succeeding fountain. Left: Years of neglect have not spoiled the architectural integrity of this unique Roman garden whose columns were imported from France.

Responding to abundant spring rains, decades old wisteria (left) displays its vibrant colors. A garden sentiment wrought in iron (above), this poem is one of innumerable treasures scattered throughout Las Tejas.

CASA DEL HERRERO

One of the principal distinctions between a formal Italian garden and a Spanish garden is the manipulation of the vision. Although divided into separate garden rooms, the Italian landscape invariably contains one long unobstructed open vista, from which other garden rooms may radiate. In the Spanish garden, this long open space is segmented, so that from one end the view is from room to room to room. In this way the Spanish garden informs the open space with a sense of mystery. Like a story unfolding chapter by chapter, the garden is traversed room by room, each area revealing new surprises. George Washington Smith, who designed the residence at Casa del Herrero, saw this difference between Italian and Spanish gardens as being precisely the difference between formality and intimacy in a garden setting.

The gardens of Casa del Herrero, for years considered one of the principal floral showplaces in Montecito, were a collaborative effort among some of the era's best landscape designers. Ralph T. Stevens and Peter Riedel developed the major garden plans, while Francis Underhill and Lockwood de Forest, more abstract in their approaches, were called upon to make later changes. George Steedman, the owner of the property and a gardening perfectionist himself, also had a hand in the design and choice of plantings. Steedman also designed and built garden furniture consistent with the name of the property, which means "House of the Blacksmith."

The garden plan starts at the residence itself, with a series of walled courtyards, each with a different floral pattern in tiles and plantings. The entrance courtyard, with its black and white pebble paving, is said to be reminiscent of the Patio de la Reja at the Alhambra in Spain. At the back of the residence, a water channel set in Moorish tiles leads away from a tiled fountain in the rear courtyard and on down a sloped axis. Along this axis one is led through the series of successive garden rooms that Smith felt to be at the heart of a Spanish garden. Bordering trees create a shaded allee the length of the water channels. Halfway down the axis is a second fountain, set in its own courtyard room. As in the courtyards set along the perimeter of the residence, this mid-level garden area features Steedman's primitive furniture. The final area on this axis is a desert-scape; a sand-floored cactus and succulent garden.

Each of the gardens at Casa del Herrero incorporate many magnificent Spanish carvings and tiles in addition to Steedman's metal garden furniture. This ornamentation enhances the intimacy for which this garden was designed. Though less ostentatious than some of the more elaborate formal Italian gardens, the Spanish-themed gardens of Casa del Herrero are spectacular in their own right. 🌿

An olla and a Spanish iron gate are an invitation to the sand-floored cactus and succulent garden beyond.

Colorful ceramic tiles were used in abundance in architect George Washington Smith's *interpretation of a Spanish garden. Decorative tiled fountains, walls and sculptures are a recurring theme in several of the courtyards at Casa del Herrero.*

Left: Arching branches of interlocking Dragon Trees (Dracaena draco) stand guard over the remains of a once-thriving desert-scape. Above: Much of the outdoor furniture and ironwork was constructed on the property by George Steedman.

VAL VERDE

Another of the estates in Montecito attesting to Lockwood de Forest's reputation as a flamboyant and avant-garde garden designer is Val Verde. When this property was first acquired by Charles H. Ludington, it consisted principally of a large boxy Mediterranean country house set on a knoll, with a view of the ocean angled off from the living and dining rooms of the villa.

The property, then called Dias Felices, or "Happy Days," had rather traditional landscaping, including a formal rose garden, sloping grassy terraces and a large Italianate reflecting pool. Below the pool meandered Montecito Creek and acres of undeveloped wooded land, criss-crossed with a series of paths. This wooded area was dense with coastal live oaks, giant Monterey cypress, sycamores, palms, olive trees, black acacias, and eucalyptus, as well as a collection of citrus trees.

When Wright Ludington inherited the property, almost immediately he renamed the estate Val Verde, or "Green Valley," and set to work with Lockwood de Forest to add interest and distinction to what Ludington felt were boring grassy slopes. Under de Forest's direction, the undistinguished grassy terraces were delineated and confirmed with the use of concrete walls and edgings, including a formal set of terraced steps leading down to the reflecting pool. The landing, just before the final descent to the pool, is adorned with a balustrade, below which a lion's head spits out a stream of water.

The terraces were further embellished by de Forest's signature geometric hedges. In this case, two parallel sets of boxwood were planted along the entire southeast face of the residence. Waist high, they extend almost three hundred feet in a continuous line broken only by the stairway leading to the reflecting pool. Between the parallel rows de Forest planted juniper, providing subtle undulating shades of green and grey-green down the slope. The collective composition of boxwood and juniper lends formality and dignity to the reflecting pool below. Additionally, these plantings visually join the upper and lower stretches of the property.

By adding geometrically precise terrace plantings, de Forest subtly extended the architecture of the residence. At the same time, by drawing attention outward from the house and on down to the reflecting pool, he enlarged the entire scope of the garden. From any point of reference the parameters of view were now expanded; house and garden were blended into a scene that encompassed both.

To complete the visual transition from house to garden, and to create a sense of wholeness to the picture, de Forest contributed one final unifying element. His stroke of genius at Val Verde, certainly his most distinctive legacy to the property, is a double row of architectural columns, square and absolutely without adornment, on both sides of the back face of the residence.

The columns are approximately twelve feet high reaching skyward, with no roof, perhaps suggesting support for the heavens above. Through the years, a number of different interpretations have been given to these double sets of roofless columns. Some say they represent decay among the ruins. Others believe they are a reference to classical Greek and Roman temples, in keeping with Ludington's noted collection of classic Greek and Roman statuary. In any case, they work extremely well as a visual metaphor, guiding the eye along from the reflecting pool and upward, toward a view of the forest beyond.

In 1928, Lockwood de Forest was hired to "add interest and distinction" to what the owner felt were "boring grassy slopes" leading to the reflecting pools. His design resulted in the attractive use of parallel rows of Juniper tamarisii folia, Japanese boxwood parterres and descending terrace steps.

De Forest's bold gamble with design culminated in the construction of these unadorned columns, which mimic the architecture of the house.

This romantic view of a sunlit fountain could easily be mistaken for an Old World Mediterranean courtyard. Left: Vertical columns and horizontal hedges outlined in afternoon shadow accentuate the precise geometric patterns adding a classical feel to the gardens at Val Verde.

CONSTANTIA

The gardens designed by Lockwood de Forest for estate properties in Montecito were diverse. Although each contained elements that were distinctly de Forest—boxwood hedges, use of native plant materials, effective use of water—each was also uniquely designed to complement the residence it adorned, such as the gardens he designed for Constantia.

The acreage at Constantia is small compared to neighboring estates; formal Italian gardens, large sweeps of lawn and meandering lengths of water channel would be impractical. Even the legendary ingenuity of de Forest was challenged to accommodate within a compact area a number of different functions: a ceremonial drive, an entrance and service court, an open area for an outdoor living room, as well as traditional parterre and flower gardens.

Integrating gardens with the architecture at Constantia provided an additional challenge to de Forest. A residence designed to resemble Cecil J. Rhodes' home in South Africa, Constantia was built in the distinctive Dutch style found in Capetown. It features six prominent gables, each decorated with a scroll pattern and topped with the image of a shell. Clearly, its architecture is among the most dramatic in Montecito. In keeping with its importance, de Forest abstracted the decorative building motifs and incorporated them into the garden, principally by sculpting the hedges, walls, and terraces in the same elaborate, curving gable form. To further extend the architectural details, he edged the flower beds with a repetitive scalloped pattern etched in cement, and then replicated this motif in scallop pavers surrounding the house.

When de Forest first approached this project, a dry creekbed spread across the northern part of the property. Rather than fill in this area, de Forest widened it, creating two ponds of different sizes. Each of the pools contains a fountain that propels water skyward. The larger of the two is home to approximately two dozen geese and swans. The simple formality of the two pools in this otherwise compact garden adds dimension to the layout. They provide not only a sense of openness and space but also ever-changing reflections of the multiple moods of sky, trees, and buildings. The pools are surrounded by sculpted hedges and oversized geometric forms crafted to imitate the distinctive Capetown architecture, and to keep all the elements of the garden in scale.

On the west side of the house is a small walled garden, with a statue of Primavera as the central focusing theme. The walls of the garden echo the roofline of the residence. Connecting this walled garden with the southern side of the property is a small sunken garden, which lies next to the house. Originally planted with a collection of African and Transvaal daisies, it now contains an arrangement of agapanthus, bird of paradise, calla lilies, and various succulents, all shaded by oaks.

When the current owners of Constantia acquired the property in 1976, they found the estate suffering from many years of neglect. The house was a dirt-streaked white, the parterres and hedges were grossly misshapen. No fountains existed, and much of the topiary had died. Undaunted, they set about restoring the property to a state of refined elegance. They extended the garden by adding to the terracing and the lower brick steps on the north face of the house and removed the holed, emaciated parterre hedging at the end of the pond. In place of this mid-range element of focus, four statues of Roman maidens were added, each representing one of the four seasons. An astute change to the garden was the addition of six palm trees on both sides of the top of the terraces that lead from the house down to the pool. From the point of view of the residence, these palm trees perfectly frame the vista of the Santa Ynez Mountains to the north.

Unwittingly, the considerate owners of Constantia perpetuate into the closing years of this century one of the themes originally intended by de Forest for this garden: a balance between immediate, mid-range and longer views. In this way, the integrity of the original design is preserved with a sense of harmony and proportion in every direction. 🌱

The current owners of Constantia astutely added the six foreground palms (Arecastrum romanzoffianum) which enhance Lockwood de Forest's idea of incorporating short, mid-range, and long vistas into the design.

A serpentine concrete gable winds toward an upper balcony which is set among the treetops of mature oaks and sycamores. Right: Three of the four Roman maidens representing the seasons stand among hedges of plumbago.

The stone statue of Primavera, recently imported from Italy, stands among a
variety of annuals in the enclosed garden on the west side of the residence.
Untamed Hedra helix nearly obscures one of Constantia's century-old
lanterns (inset).

A residence designed to resemble Cecil J. Rhodes' home in South Africa, Constantia was built in the distinctive Dutch style found in Capetown in the nineteenth century.

Clivia bloom behind Japanese boxwood in a planting bed edged with cement scallops typical of those found throughout the estate. Left: Alyssum, impatiens, Mandevilla splendens, and kalanchoe are set in planter boxes under the foyer windows in colors which complement the warm hues of the residence.

ISOLA BELLA

Another of the estates that has gracefully made the transition from the nineteenth into the twentieth century is Isola Bella. The property was once part of a larger estate owned by landscape architect Charles F. Eaton, who had acquired it from the family of fabled nurseryman Kinton Ralph Stevens. The residence at Isola Bella was built in 1911-1912 by the daughter of John Doe, Marguerite Doe Rogers Courtney Ravenscroft, who obtained the estate from Eaton's daughter.

Ms. Doe lived at Isola Bella only briefly after the residence was constructed, though she and her estate held the property for a cumulative forty-three years. The peripatetic lifestyle of Ms. Doe did not allow for the commitment necessary to develop the property, and it wasn't until recently that Isola Bella received the time and attention necessary to realize its potential.

When the current owners of Isola Bella acquired the property in 1983, extensive remodeling and landscape design work had already been undertaken. They have continued and expanded upon this previous work, expending massive amounts of time and effort to create an immaculate showplace. The original residence has been extensively remodelled and a service house has been renovated as a gatehouse. Designed by Michael De Rose with a Siennese, Italian influence to complement the main residence, the gatehouse serves as the owner's office and as additional quarters for guests.

The greatest transformation at Isola Bella, however, is in the gardens. Drawing on formal Italian references in keeping with the architecture and historical significance of the estate, the gardens at Isola Bella have been adapted to contemporary lifestyles.

The entrance to the estate is through what was once the service entrance, with large iron gates also specially designed by De Rose to complement the residence and its formal gardens. The newly restored and expanded gatehouse is bordered by a small, formal parterre garden; dwarf citrus trees, in proportion to the parterre, grow between the hedges. The parterres are in a double-X formation and are flanked with drought-tolerant plantings along the edge of the drive.

The drive into the estate terminates in a parking circle in front of the formal lemon-washed Italianate house, marked by tall stands of strelitzia. Opposite the main entrance and across the circular drive sit two large cat sculptures, flanking a pathway that leads through an old-fashioned olive allee to an undulating, free-form pool gracing the southeast corner of the property. The backdrop of the pool area echoes the lushness of the central part of the garden.

Drawing back from the pool and on around to the side of the residence are three oaks, each standing thirty to forty feet high, with branches spreading at some points as much as fifty feet. These great oaks shade the balance of the lawn which stretches around the northeastern boundaries of the residence. On the western side of the property, the main residence is connected to the gatehouse by a formal rose garden, with a path from the residence under a trellis displaying a white Copa de Oro vine. When the front door of the main residence is open, one can look straight through the house to view a small keyhole garden and bird bath. Topiary borders the entry to this cloistered garden, which is surrounded by a wall of used brick.

With the dedicated efforts of the current owners, perfect harmony now reigns between the house and gardens of Isola Bella, truly making it the "beautiful isle" promised by its name ❧

Siennese Italian influences predominate on this Michael De Rose–designed architecture. Right: Don Quixote sculpture by Willis Baldwin is set in a bed of Santa Barbara daisies. In the background is an Australian Tea Tree.

Montecito's year-round temperate climate is ideally suited for inviting the outdoors in. Although indoors, these sixteenth century Chinese wood carvings blend gracefully with the Australian tree ferns and into the garden scene beyond.

Staghorn fern thrive under the broad canopies of these immaculately groomed California live oaks. The practice of pruning interior branches from oaks, creating an umbrella of upper leaves, began in the 1920s and has since become known among local arborists as the Montecito trim.

PIRANHURST

Of the early Montecito estates that capitalized on the views of mountains and ocean, perhaps none has done so as brilliantly as Piranhurst. The three-story residence, built of concrete with a plaster exterior, sits high on a knoll at the foot of the Santa Ynez Mountains with a commanding view in all directions. From the residence southward, a great lawn, punctuated with magnificent oaks, opens out toward an uninterrupted view of the Pacific Ocean. To the north, the ubiquitous mountains cast their imposing shadow over the property.

The extensive formal gardens were laid out in cooperation between the original owners and J. Wilkinson Elliott, a noted Pittsburg landscape architect. So beautiful was the execution of Elliott's design that by the early 1930s, Piranhurst was described as "one of the best planted places in Montecito Valley."

From the terrace on the south side of the property, steps sweep toward the formal gardens below. Cascading down from the terrace, the principal portion of the garden is comprised of a massive lawn, tapering down a slope over a hundred yards to the south and extending over two hundred yards in width. This area is the largest private green belt in Montecito and is rimmed with stands of oak, under which flourish a profusion of agapanthus, geranium, impatiens, Iceland poppies and other seasonal flowers. Croquet games are played out on the lower, more level area of the lawn from which the view back up the hill reveals the south face of the residence, draped in the shocking pink hues of flowering bougainvillea.

The west side of the property makes dramatic and clever use of a natural creekbed. A large sunken garden with an outdoor Greek Theater was built at one end, where Italian cypress hedges at one time formed six sections of boxes for the spectators. For many years, the theater was written about in numerous garden magazines. It was also depicted on local postcards, and social events utilizing the theater were often featured in the society pages of local papers.

The current owners of Piranhurst have extended the natural line of the original streambed, constructing a meandering creek above the outdoor amphitheater garden. The newly formed creekbed is lined with local stone and fed by an automated recycling watering system that insures a flowing creek on demand.

Throughout the property, elegant statuary has been discretely placed. Wandering down a wooded path, tucked under a tree, or turning a corner of a flowering bed the statuary constantly surprises, echoing the essential formality of these grounds.

Stunning vistas, sweeping lawns, stands of magnificent trees, and sculptured garden areas combine to make this property one of the finest private estates found anywhere. Piranhurst is truly grand in every sense of the word. 🌿

Tasmanian and Australian tree ferns surround this life-size Roman statue on the interior of the motorcourt.

Throughout the spring Montecito is frequented by fog which diffuses the morning sun, adding a softness to the landscape.

Years of meticulous grooming leave the impression that this expansive use of Creeping fig stands unsupported as it drapes the ten-foot motorcourt walls.

The lawns of Piranhurst are its most dramatic feature. Covering over a quarter million square feet and dotted with magnificent oaks, this front yard view is Montecito's largest privately owned park.

Watsonia (above and right).

This cutting garden, reminiscent of those found at Italian villas, was intentionally placed to take full advantage of southern exposure.

GARDENS FOR OUTDOOR LIVING

Gardens have always provided an opportunity to enjoy nature, to rejuvenate the spirit, or simply to savor a place of beauty—and garden design has evolved to encourage these activities. In the ancient world, Grecian parks, Islamic water gardens and Medieval walled courtyards all included walks, arbors, benches and colonnades as inducements to patronage. Even the most formal Italian Renaissance gardens with their various garden "rooms" were designed to be walked in as well as viewed from a distance.

In Montecito, as in most of Southern California, the concept of a garden as a firsthand experience has been gradually expanded to incorporate living out-of-doors. Wealthy families who arrived here from the East Coast around the turn of the century recreated gardens similar to those they had enjoyed at home: formal gardens designed not even for walking, but for viewing only. As a result of Montecito's temperate climate, however, a change of sensibility occurred and people became more comfortable with the idea of spending time outdoors. They even developed new, often whimsical, and sometimes flamboyant ways of enjoying themselves, such as building funiculars for transportation to mountain tea houses, amphitheaters to present theatrical and musical events, and miniature lakes to accommodate their boats. They developed gardens around croquet and tennis

courts, with special pergolas allowing shaded spectators to enjoy the games.

Later, as the transition to outdoor living became an end in itself, garden design evolved to reflect the way people conducted their daily lives. What is now called the "Southern California lifestyle" is actually a warm-weather way of life similar to that enjoyed in Mexico, Hawaii, Spain, Africa and the Mediterranean region—all areas where people have traditionally spent much of their leisure time outdoors.

The architecture and gardens of these countries demonstrate how distinctions between outdoors and indoors blend and fade. Food is prepared on outdoor grills or barbecue pits and eaten on lanais or patios. Work is often carried on outdoors, and outdoor sports include the whole family. On warm nights, people may sleep outside on porches intended for that purpose. Many of these warm-weather conventions were adopted in the house and garden designs of Southern California.

After World War II, the notion of designing gardens to embrace everyday outdoor activities found an advocate in landscape designer Thomas Church. Church had a tremendous influence on the direction of California landscape design. His gardens honored the decision of post–World War II homeowners to incorporate Southern California sunshine into their lifestyles. Stylized lawns, formal parterres and tidy perennial borders gave way to terraces, outdoor barbecues, swimming pools with cabanas, and play areas for children.

Over time, the expansive Montecito estates of yesteryear have been outnumbered by modest estates on limited acreage. The gardens of these smaller estates adapt traditional designs to their space limitations and echo the trend of including outdoor lifestyle features. Italian garden design is typical of this adaptation: lawns are still used, but now they are terraced; formal rose gardens are placed on steps; paths are used to level a sloping property; and parterres, though smaller, still convey an air of dignity. Overall, the restrained use of familiar landscaping features creates the same sense of peacefulness and privacy experienced in much larger gardens.

When Spanish colonial architecture gained popularity in Montecito with the designs of George Washington Smith, attention turned toward creating complementary gardens. Landscape architects used this trend as a springboard to break free from the Italian tradition. The less ostentatious Spanish gardens are typically smaller in size and include a series of connected semi-enclosed garden areas, often decorated with tile or ironwork. Garden benches and other furniture encourage the leisurely enjoyment of outdoor life.

Similarly, masterpieces of English and French country architecture provide the perfect backdrop for small cottage gardens. Brimming with colorful flowers, these gardens are perfectly at home amidst the native oaks and sycamores. Other garden treasures of Montecito adorn Craftsman-era homes, which, with their reliance on unembellished natural materials, blend seamlessly into the terrain at the foot of the Santa Ynez Mountains. These traditional gardens are the perfect backdrop for swimming pools, tennis courts, and other contemporary living features that are heirs of the Church legacy.

Freed from the rigid adherence to traditional landscape design, Montecito's modern gardens for outdoor living are sometimes irregular in form, with spaces that flow from one area of activity to the next. But this does not imply random or capricious design. These gardens possess a sense of balance that reflects both the architecture of the house and the site. They enhance the natural landscape rather than alter it to fit a preconceived design. Trees, boulders, gullies and other landmarks are retained wherever possible. Low maintenance plantings are increasingly used in these gardens.

In Montecito gardens today, distinctions between

house as functional space and garden as backdrop or setting are less obvious than ever before. With a climate that invites year-round activity, outdoor garden "rooms" become as important as rooms inside the home—and when outdoor areas incorporate the same materials used in the residence, even the visual distinctions blur. The garden becomes an extension of the home, expressing the unique grace and beauty for which Montecito is known the world over. 🌿

A sculpture created by Marge Dunlap.

In 1956, Lutah Maria Riggs designed "Hesperides" for philanthropist Wright Ludington. Classic in design, it was ideally placed in the midst of an olive grove in the eastern foothills of Montecito. The garden was created by landscape architect Elizabeth de Forest. The third and current owners of the property have restored the original design themes of Riggs and de Forest.
Right: Over six feet in height, this two hundred year old French urn, which shattered upon its arrival in Los Angeles, has been painstakingly reassembled and placed in the olive grove.

The southwestern edge of the garden pavilion offers a captivating view of the Montecito Valley, Santa Barbara and the Channel Islands beyond.

A half dozen male albino peacocks roam freely. Visitors are frequently privileged to witness their simultaneous display of fanned white plumage.

A large bathing pool below the house reflects the surrounding landscape. Inset: Bronze statuary conveys an air of classic beauty. Left: French lavender, a favorite of de Forest, has been planted en masse.

Ranunculi and California poppies fill an English field-style garden in the heart of Montecito. An authentic replica of a French Normandy country home, the residence was built in the post—World War I era by a veteran who was nursed back to health in France and fell in love with the countryside there. The present owners have created an oasis of varied gardens, largely English in style.

The kitchen and dining area of the home overlook a display of
brilliant gerberas and roses, and beyond to the cottage garden.
Inset: The Star of Bethlehem, indigenous to South Africa, bears
these showy blooms in early summer.

Baby Tears and lobelia spread across a cobbled brick walk at the front entrance of the home. Inset: The delicate blooms of Rose campion (Lychnis coronaria) are visited by a Monarch butterfly. Right: Foxglove, larkspur, roses, iris, perennial flax and daffodils are among the profusion of flowers in this spectacular English-style garden.

Designed by George Washington Smth in 1923, this estate has incorporated the contemporary landscape design of Isabelle Greene. A lush garden at the rear of the house (above) includes Siberian iris, foxglove, delphinium, white watsonia, and artemisia. Right: The unique swimming pool, surrounded by natural stone, blends perfectly into the tree-shaded surroundings. A nearby Japanese tea house serves as a bath house for the pool.

One of Montecito's fine historic estates, Villa Reposa, was built in 1916 to resemble a manor house near Lake Como in Italy. A stand of fiery Aloe arborescens adjoins the estate's formal hedges and lawns. Left: This simple wrought iron bench extends an invitation to enjoy the garden's deep shade.

The pink blooms of a Jade plant and an arch of Creeping fig surround this classic lion's head. Right: In a pleasing display of whites, pinks, and reds, this shaded flower bed includes Silver Lady marguerites, roses, alyssum and the red flowering cigar plant.

Harold Gladwin, an Englishman and prominent Montecito resident, purchased this estate in 1938 and named it "The Green Hill." He employed the famed Hollywood landscape designer Florence Yoch to create the original garden design. Updated by Isabelle Greene, the garden today offers a pleasing display of color year-round. In early spring, this bed includes spiraea, forget-me-nots, tulips and columbine. At the rear is a large pink jasmine bush. Inset: Flowering peach blossom.

Over 50 years old, this Japanese wisteria vine was carefully removed from the home's original garage and placed on its own scaffolding while the new house was under construction. *Left: This stone and tile fountain is one of the few pieces on the grounds which dates from Florence Yoch's work on the property. The steps, pathways and rock work were fashioned by Isabelle Greene to complement the remaining elements of Yoch's design.*

Built in 1918, Ca' di Sopra is an outstanding example of an authentic Italian villa. It was designed by Guy Lowell, who at the time was one of the two foremost experts on Italian design in this country. (The other was Addison Mizner, architect of Casa Bienvenida.) Ca' di Sopra is the only representation of Lowell's work on the West Coast. The hillside grounds cover six acres and are a treasure trove of Italianate detail.

Ca' di Sopra is divided into two levels: the upper level with main house and gardens, and the wooded lower level with a clearing for family picnics. A 300 ft. funicular was installed to join them, providing easy access to gatherings held below. The single cable car, marked by the number 7, still runs today.

Fast-growing Sedum morganianum, more commonly known as Donkey's tail, spills over its pot on the garden grounds.

Set in the foothills at the top of a long, winding drive, this contemporary estate incorporates the best of traditional Italian design. Fountains and statuary framed by colorful flowers create a distinctive atmosphere of grace and beauty. Left: Plantings in the spacious motorcourt include Italian cypress and white ivy geranium. The cross-hatching is filled with dwarf hybrid Bermuda grass.

This George Washington Smith estate was built in 1924 for James R. H. Wagner, one of the founding members of the Montecito Community Association. Today the magnificent grounds feature a rock waterfall and pond-shaped swimming pool, tennis courts, and an outdoor eating area with old-fashioned brick barbecue. Sweeping lawns, bright flower beds, a walled meditation garden, and a walled rose garden complete this elegant estate. Above: Known as a living fossil, Gingko biloba with its unique fan-shaped leaves dates back to Mesozoic times. Its seed kernels have medicinal properties.

The owners of this seventeenth-century English Tudor bought the house in England, and reconstructed it in this idyllic Montecito setting. This verdant English knot garden incorporates Japanese boxwood hedges, roses, citrus trees, and rose scented geraniums. Impatiens bloom under the kitchen window. Right: The sunny breakfast room looks out to a brick-walled garden lush with white roses.

Santa Barbara daisies and Holly ferns surround natural boulders on the way to a rustic pavilion, perfect for year-round entertaining.

A weathered brick patio is punctuated by heliotrope-filled hedges.

The grounds of Fairleigh, an estate whose Craftsman-era residence was designed by Bernard Maybeck, feature towering California live oaks and majestic views of the Santa Ynez Mountains. Adirondack chairs overlook a rose garden and a picturesque grove of olive trees.

When Ronald Colman, star of the silent screen, became co-owner of Montecito's San Ysidro Ranch in the 1930s, he purchased a nearby estate known as Verbois. There he built a new residence, which he named Random House. Today the estate retains some of the original landscape features designed by Lockwood de Forest. *Left: The back terrace boasts a view of the swimming pool. Below: Brilliant hibiscus surround the estate's koi pond. Right: Afternoon light glows against this mosaic of local stone.*

This unique residence and garden, currently being restored by its owners, were designed by Lutah Maria Riggs. Japanese boxwood hedges and English ivy, arranged in perfect symmetry, contribute to the stately, dignified atmosphere.

The deep green of tall Italian cypress lines the façade of El Retiro. Dating back to 1926, the estate was designed by George Washington Smith for his good friend Henry Eichheim, a violinist with the Boston Symphony.

Casa del Greco, circa 1920, has the distinction of being the second home George Washington Smith built for himself in the Santa Barbara area. The gardens of this L-shaped residence are organized around a central vista and extensive Japanese boxwood hedges. A water channel cuts through the property. Right: A grove of black acacia, one of the signature elements of landscape design by Lockwood de Forest.

Reminiscent of an English stone cottage, Hacienda de Piedras was built by architect Carleton M. Winslow in 1918. A path on the east side of the house winds through an English country garden of perennials designed by the current owner. Lavender lantana and Swedish ivy, also known as yellow sencecio, form a showy mass of color. Inset: Repeating stone arches frame a patio with views across the treetops to the ocean below. In the pot is a vibrant Rieger begonia, a cross between the fibrous and tuberous varieties.

In spring and summer, columbine blooms in the English garden. The name columbine comes from the Latin aquila, or eagle—which refers to the curved spurs extending out behind the flowers.

Tall horsetail reeds stand in the spray of a multi-level waterfall at this historic Montecito estate. The sound of water falling at different levels acts as noise abatement for nearby East Valley Road. In the foreground are the bright purple flowers of brunfelsia.

Deep in the heart of a mystical glade is this delicate fountain, designed by Barry De Vorzon and Joshua Vaughan. Sunlight filters gently through the canopy to the grassy floor and koi pond below.

Hidden at the rear of the property, the estate's swimming pool and low waterfall are designed in harmony with nature. Varied hues of green creep straight to the water's edge.

Set on a terraced hillside with extensive recreational amenities, this sprawling Mediterranean estate delights the eye with flowers at every turn. In summer, creamy white gardenias bloom near the house, filling the air with fragrance.

Cascading down a slope from an enclosed terrace are Pink Frolic lantana and Bougainvillea 'Rosenka.'

Small, clear pools descend via terraces to a large pool at the base of the hill. The adjacent plantings include weeping birch and French lavender. In the distance are spectacular views of the valley, ocean and Channel Islands.

Carefully blending sun and shade, the swimming pool area features extensive stonework and impeccably maintained plantings. Stone steps lead to the tennis court below.

Colorful ranunculi, part of the buttercup family, are commonly seen in
Montecito planting beds during summer months. Opposite: This inviting
backyard hillside is covered with blooms, including roses, geraniums, nasturtiums
and the purple Pride of Madeira (Echium fastuosum). The same flowers fill the
vase on the table, along with irises, Calla lilies and Day lilies. French doors
that bring the outside in are an essential part of Montecito style.

Nestled on a picturesque hillside, Villa Santa Lucia was designed to evoke a Tuscan town. Landscape architect Phil Shipley took advantage of the spacious grounds and fabulous vistas to create garden areas for outdoor family living. The swimming pool and waterfall are completely surrounded by lawns, trees and flowers.

A massive rock wall is flanked by rich green grass and Bougainvillea 'Rosenka.' Above the main house, the property features a Cabernet Sauvignon vineyard and a terraced play area for children.

Fast-growing Boston ivy—a common variety in European countries—spreads across an archway at the home's main entrance. The containers below hold pink Begonia 'Richmondensis.' Right: In true Tuscan style, a high stucco wall is obscured by climbing vines, among them Bougainvillea 'San Diego Red.' The tiny yellow blossoms of Cape honeysuckle rise up from below.

The white flowers of ornamental strawberry cover the bank alongside a waterfall crafted from native stone. The water flows into a creek which gradually meanders down to the swimming pool, bath house and barbecue area. Right: Bright yellow mimulus (monkey flowers) grow along the streambed, while nearby olive trees provide refreshing shade.

Winding their way past wrought ironwork, the green leaves of Boston ivy turn
scarlet in autumn. Left: Rustic paths lead throughout the residential complex and
grounds. Here the borders are lined with grey-green santolina, whose common
name is "petal-less daisy."

Royal purple bougainvillea provides a bright spot of color in this unusually private Birnam Wood garden. The lawn is bordered by pink blooms of dwarf bedding begonia. California live oaks and blue gum eucalyptus form the shady canopy above.

Mosaic-like, a cobbled path of native stone adds the perfect country touch. Though a golf course lies just beyond the white picket fence, this garden, designed to provide its owners a measure of privacy, seems to exist in a world all its own.

At this Birnam Wood estate, horticulturalist Ray Sodomka used splashes of color to extend the spirit of Fiesta year round—among them, the bright orange blooms of Cape honeysuckle. Left: Mexican sage and red bougainvillea add a festive air to this country club garden.

Attention to detail characterizes the grounds of this large estate, which includes a horse farm, swimming pool and huge vegetable garden. Annual and perennial borders on the property are always kept in flower. In spring, pink ageratum tosses its feather-like blossoms, and purple cineraria grows up along the fence. *Right: A brilliant red Camellia japonica thrives in its favored environment: the leafy shade and mulch of a California live oak.*

Left: La Bergerie, an eloquent expression of French country charm, is set in the Montecito foothills against the backdrop of the Santa Ynez Mountains. An immense rose garden with charming weathered brick arbors extends across the front and side of the main residence. Above: At the rear of the estate, a grassy, parklike setting dotted with massive trees and statuary invites the visitor to enjoy a few moments of repose.

The breathtaking view across Santa Barbara from this east-west reflecting pool, culminates with the wharf and ocean beyond.

Plantings chosen for form and color, such as Agave attenuata (above) and bougainvillea (right), add graceful accents to a low stucco wall near the residence. Towering over the rolling lawns and shade trees are the majestic Santa Ynez Mountains.

Following Japanese principles, landscape architect Grant Castleberg created an outdoor environment in harmony with this property's contemporary residence and Oriental art collection. The striking pool and waterfall area has a terrace for outdoor dining and barbecues. Plantings include Wheeler's dwarf pittosporum, Japanese black pine, liriope and blue oat grass.

In this meditative courtyard at the front of the house, an espaliered evergreen pear spreads gracefully across a wall.

This traditionally-styled residence, reminiscent of a New England country home, features clapboard construction and "tromp l'oeil" landscaping by Sandra Devine. Skillful terracing and masses of flowers successfully disguise the steep hillside—among them, Bougainvillea 'Rosenka,' lavender lantana, blue felicia, and Martha Washington geranium. Adirondack chairs overlook the tennis court; directly behind them is the swimming pool.

A mix of color bears witness to Montecito's reputation for year-round summer.

The grounds of this Montecito family estate, designed by landscape architect Sandra Devine, display many aspects of a true outdoor lifestyle garden—from ponds and pools to play houses and lath houses. A profusion of California poppies thrives outside the lath house, which is crowned by a cup of gold vine (Solandra maxima). Left: This shaded outdoor eating area is surrounded by tranquil pools and plantings such as irises, marguerites and pink Cecil Brunner roses.

Purple irises line the path to the impressive pool, bath house and terrace, secluded under the shade of massive California live oaks.

A family of black pygmy goats grazes contentedly on thick grass in the spacious children's play area.

The Tudor façade of the house, complete with red geraniums in window boxes, overlooks a pristine lawn with pond and statuary. English garden themes are incorporated in many locations around the estate.

The creamy white flowers of Angel's trumpet vine frame this view of the children's play area and teepee. As the flowers age on the vine, they turn a yellowish hue.

At twilight, the pool house of this rambling country estate is lit like a welcoming beacon. To the left is an exercise ring for horses. Left: French doors from the breakfast room open onto this eye-catching display of color. Roses, purple solanum and Mexican sage (Salvia leucantha) are enhanced by ivy geraniums and New Guinea impatiens in clay pots.

Landscape architect Sandra Devine used green swards and flowering beds to define outdoor living areas around the estate. Here, the repeating theme of ivy geranium, roses and solanum surrounds a stone terrace. The top of the pool house can be seen to the right. *Right: Lavender lantana crowds the pasture fence to frame an idyllic pastoral scene.*

The artist's studio of Beverly Hyman-Fead brings the outdoors in through a picture window overlooking a grove of California live oak. On the easel is a scene from the estate's outdoor living room.

Cymbidiums flourish under the perfect conditions of the outdoor living room.

Hyman-Fead, a ceramicist as well as a painter, has set the table for an outdoor meal using dishes of her own design. Tulip magnolias in a glass vase add the finishing touch. The house above overlooks this expansive lawn area.

Montecito's temperate Mediterranean climate allows the outdoor living room to be used virtually year-round. The dappled shade and jasmine-scented air create a serene environment for relaxation.

NATIVE LANDSCAPES

Warm sunny days, cool evenings, mild winters—
Montecito is blessed with a Mediterranean-like climate. But the blessing is mixed. Sometimes
months or even years go by with very few inches of rain. And when the rains do come, often they
arrive in a deluge, overflowing creeks and stream beds, occasionally jeopardizing nearby gardens and
homes.

Finding ways to cope with its rainfall pattern has always been a problem for Montecito
residents. Historical accounts start with the Chumash Indians seeking to preserve and conserve
water for drinking and for irrigation of crops and gardens. By the late nineteenth century, elaborate
water channelling and drainage systems were in place, providing continuous supplies of water to the
citrus and avocado ranches dotting the Montecito landscape.

When the great estate properties, with their huge demand for water, were developed at the
beginning of this century, new solutions to the water problem were introduced. Among the more
ingenious of these were tunnels bored into the mountains to trap spring water, as well as artificial
lakes with water stairs that channeled water from cisterns in the foothills of the Santa Ynez
Mountains down to the residences below. Some properties were situated so that developers could
dig wells and tap into the water table underground.

Montecito gardeners have had no choice but to design around the problem of a fluctuating

*Aloe thraskii are surrounded by Rosea ice plant which bloom in early spring. Used as hillside
ground cover, its shocking magenta color can be seen from miles away.*

Purple Ceanothus (wild lilac) grows in two varieties: groundcover and shrub. Normally deciduous, it responds favorably to Montecito's temperate climate and may bloom several times a year.

supply of water. Whatever the garden style, designers looked to drought tolerant species to provide color and diversity that in other areas might be provided by seasonal varieties. Thanks to the pioneering work of men such as Kinton Ralph Stevens, Peter Riedel and Francesco Franceschi, landscape designers in the first part of this century had ready access to tropical and subtropical varieties that had already been proven to grow abundantly in Santa Barbara's climate on a minimum of water. To be truthful, designers began using these materials less out of environmental concern than as a matter of practicality. They still used traditional elements such as vast lawns that guzzled water when it was plentiful, and dried out when water was scarce.

But garden styles change over time, and so does the environmental consciousness of a community. Today, there is widespread commitment to create gardens that are not only beautiful but are also friendly to the environment. The style of these gardens aptly could be called creative landscaping, with emphasis on the "creative." Just because it conserves water, a garden need not be staid or boring. Designers discovered that the key to successful water conscious garden design is to select plant materials for their low water requirements and their capacity to adapt naturally to the micro-climate of a specific site. As some of the water-efficient landscapes in Montecito clearly show, there is ample opportunity for creativity within the confines of drought tolerant conditioning.

Drought tolerant gardening brings many rewards in addition to its beauty. Creating outdoor environments that echo the natural world not only conserves precious resources, but reduces hands-on maintenance. Despite the region's periodic droughts, Montecito has its own brand of lushness, and the prevailing climate has made this community a perfect testing ground for pushing the limits of creativity in water efficient gardening styles. ❦

Morning fog is a typical spring weather condition in the valley. The captured dampness highlights the delicate features of plant life and, in this photograph, the exquisite beauty of the web.

The needles of the yellow-thorned Notocactus sparkle in the morning sun.

A hillside collection of oleander, lantana, Mexican sage and Euphorbia ingens is a composite of color, texture and shape.

A burst of Wheeler's sotel and towering Euphorbia ingens complement the simplicity of Southwestern styled architecture.

Agave attenuata in late bloom arch over the statue of Our Lady of Mount Carmel (left). The church of Our Lady of Mount Carmel, built in 1936, is a well known Montecito landmark. Frequently photographed, the church and its grounds (above) have been landscaped exclusively in drought tolerant species.

The Arco Corporation commissioned artist Herbert Bayer to create a colorful tile sculpture within a reflecting pool at their Montecito corporate retreat (left). Recirculating water, selective use of lawn, and colorful plants like the Blue hibiscus and bougainvillea "Rosenka" give the impression of lushness.

In an effort to reduce water usage, many Montecito homeowners have begun to substitute water conscious plants without sacrificing visual appeal. Here, pennisetum and New Zealand flax have been incorporated into a hillside garden. Clivia (inset) is a colorful alternative for water thirsty plants used in shaded bedding areas .

Meditation stones have been placed on a slab of local stone. Purple hopseed surround this restful setting.

Vegetables, flowers and succulents thrive in adjoining beds in this Isabelle Greene-designed garden (left). Snow in summer, Kleinia, Guatemalan sedum, and three species of agave are seen in an overhead view of this landscape designed to simulate the patchwork of farmlands (below).

Crassula

Above: A warm mosaic of stone creates a fluid look as it meanders through groupings of drought tolerant plantings. "Rosenka" (inset) and other colorful species of bougainvillea are among the valley's most popular plants. Right: A courtyard pond is the only obvious display of water in an otherwise conservation-minded garden. The clever recirculating system is segregated from beds that contain water thrifty plants.

Eight varieties of unrelated drought tolerant plants take on a similar grey-green cast in full shade.

Left: Spanish dagger, a common yucca, thrives in open sun and sandy soil. Its bi-annual bloom and soft green hues make it the ideal complement to Mediterranean architecture. Right: Imported olive trees and the creative use of plant variety give this nearly new garden an established feel.

This early evening image of cacti and cereus could easily be mistaken for a Southwestern desert scene.

PHOTOGRAPHY

STEVE ELTINGE

front cover, back cover, dust flap, 2, 5, 6 bottom, 7 middle, 7 bottom, 8, 10, 11, 14, 21, 24, 25, 26, 27, 28, 29, 30, 31, 34, 35, 37, 38, 42, 46, 48, 49, 53, 55, 57, 58, 59, 60, 61, 63, 64, 67, 69, 74, 75 top, 76, 78, 79, 81, 82, 84, 85, 86, 87, 91, 92, 93, 95, 96, 97 bottom, 98, 99, 103 bottom, 105, 106, 109, 110, 112, 114, 115, 117, 119, 120, 125, 126, 127, 128, 136, 139, 143, 144, 146, 148, 149, 150, 151, 152, 153, 154, 156, 157, 158, 159, 160, 162, 164, 166, 167, 168, 169, 170, 171, 172, 173, 174, 175, 176, 177, 179, 186, 187, 188, 189, 191 top, 192, 193, 195, 196 inset, 199, 200, 201, 202, 203, 204, 206, 207, 208, 209, 212, 213, 214, 215, 218, 219, 220, 222, 223, 224, 225, 226, 227, 228, 229, 230, 231, 232, 233, 234, 235, 236, 237, 238, 239, 240, 241, 242, 243, 248, 249, 250, 253, 254, 257, 261, 262, 263, 264, 265, 266, 267, 268, 269, 270, 271, 273 top, 274, 275.

MARIO E. QUINTANA

1, 4, 6 top, 7 top, 12, 16, 23, 32, 33, 36, 40, 45, 50, 51, 52, 56, 66, 70, 71, 72, 73, 75 inset, 80, 88, 94, 97 inset, 100, 101, 102, 103 top, 104, 111, 113, 116, 118, 121, 122, 123, 124, 129, 130, 132, 133, 134, 135, 140, 141, 142, 145, 178, 180, 181, 182, 183, 184, 185, 190, 191 inset, 194, 196 top, 197, 198, 205, 210, 211, 216, 217, 221, 244, 245, 246, 247, 251, 258, 259, 260, 272, 273 bottom.